OPEN WORKINGS

D1189119

Also by Iain Bamforth from Carcanet

Sons and Pioneers

IAIN BAMFORTH

OPEN WORKINGS

CARCANET

First published in 1996 by
Carcanet Press Limited
402-406 Corn Exchange Buildings
Manchester M4 3BY

A CIP catalogue record for this book
is available from the British Library
ISBN 1 85754 257 6

The publisher acknowledges financial assistance
from the Arts Council of England

Set in 10 pt Bembo by Bryan Williamson, Frome
Printed and bound in England by SRP Ltd, Exeter

The shortest distance between two points is not always a straight line

Nikolai Lobachevski 1792-1856

Acknowledgements and Notes

Acknowledgements are due to the editors of the following periodicals in which some of these poems first appeared: *Poetry Review, Gairfish, la Traductière* (France), *Quadrant* (Australia) and *PN Review*. Earlier versions of 'Mountains and Valleys', 'The Country Called Commitment', 'A Clear Thought', 'The Water Tower' and 'The Ice Factory' were published as a contribution to the *PN Review* hundredth edition, *A Calendar of Modern Poetry* (1994).

'Going Out' expands an abandoned sextet of 1914 in the Rilke *Nachlaß*: 'Der Landschaft Liebe'. 'Unsystematic Anatomy' adopts the Rabelaisian list method, first used to preposterously good effect in Chapter 30 of *le Quart Livre* – 'Comment par Xenomanes est anatomisé et descript Quaresmeprenant'. 'Impediments' is a civil construction site of the Mitterrand years which requires hard hats. 'Up and Down the Ayr Road' is a Burns bicentenary poem which also brings Keats – 'Ay, on the shores of darkness there is light,/And precipices show untrodden green' (*To Homer*) and Defoe back to the stretch of what is now the A77 from Ballantrae to Ayr.

David Rorie's admirable but largely unnoticed *Folk Tradition and Folk Medicine in Scotland* (Canongate, Edinburgh, 1994) supplied me with the background information for several poems, along with a clear view of the historical origins and contestable nature of a doctor's 'apostolic' function in a small community; and a refrain in his friend Carmichael's *Carmina Gadelica* worked as structural model for the charm in 'Between the Rhins and the Machars'. 'The ear hears more/Than any tongue' comes from W.S. Graham's poem 'The Hill of Intrusion' and could stand as a motto for the view of the doctor, patient and illness embraced in 'Doing Calls on the Old Portpatrick Road'. William Osler in 'A Small Exchange of Air' was a famous (and influential) clinician at the beginning of the century still remembered for his volume 'Aequanimitas'; Asher in 'Sympathetic Healing' is another physician best known to general practitioners for his pithy 'Talking Sense'. The line 'the working life as a matter of conscience and (a matter of) faith in one's fellow man' in 'Subjects and Objects' is taken from Kafka's report for the Workers' Accident Insurance Institute *Commune of Workers without Private Property* (1918).

The quotation from Auden at the beginning of 'A Hole in the World' comes from an early verse play 'The Chase' (1934). 'Gob Road' fits around a term from the earth sciences: to gob is to pack a seam with debris after excavation in order to prevent collapse.

Contents

Mountains and Valleys

> And now it was time for me to think of escaping
> Kafka, *A Country Doctor*

Once I had gone into the low adobes
from the mountains and valleys
everything became obvious;
faces hid in hands,
there was a spreading dimness
and quiet turning away, and I heard
a final warning about the man
with a mind of his own.

That day my name was Mud.
A brotherhood of stove-pipe hats
huddled me across the verdict
and onto commonsense's level ground,
downwind from the tannery
and the biblical beasts of burden.
What was on my mind
was the fate of my Gladstone.

And then they smiled, wanting
to teach me who I was.
Folk history, it's a hempen bind
and hedgehog diffidence
but the good book on the trestle
said I hadn't heard the half.
When I talked of leaving
it made as much sense to stay.

December blew off the river
and they weren't what they seemed,
the mountains and valleys.
Hands delved for dishes,
the dark route through the day.
All I heard was aftermath –
gutters adept with rain,
slow openings after, brimmings.

The Country Called Commitment

There's no way back
along the rutted lanes and puddles
where light settles
into a final liquefaction
of its natural uses.

Will tomorrow come?
None of us knows for certain
or cares enough to ask.
Flakes of sky dwindle down
on the one square plot.

There's only the wind
brushing blackly on the door.
It lifts the house up
slightly, like the hem of a skirt.
It claims the usual stakes.

Heifers get off their haunches.
Day stands in the door.
No other way to go but back
to hope and haunting
who's home and who's not.

Going Out

after Rilke

Time and again we go out, hope in our heads,
though we know each bield and outhouse
in the landscape of love, rows of granite terraces

with their rhones and gables, the mercat cross
looking slackly down on what it means to be
home, fresh-puffed-up clouds amassing

time and again, though we know the poky
vandalised kirk and its attitudinising messenger,
pitfalls and flacks and sporting shibboleths

appointed to guy us, still we go out
hand in hand, imminent in a crowd of kids
and flapping parents, to the improbably giant

fossilized trees where we rest for the duration,
coats off in the bracken, ogling the sky.

The Ice Factory

When the breath of danger finally fades
dawn is one more broken vessel.
'Trace it back to where it came from –
what you'll come away with is vertigo and malaise.'

Outside a small ceremony's taking place
under eerie noonday lightning,
the life-symbol glazing to a durable icon.
'Just leave it for the cleaners in the morning.'

Even in this white place, intelligence slowly
pulls out leaves from its bare sleeves.
Overhead a petrel raises the alarm,
and we go in behind the bulwarks of silence.

A row of tents drags on its sinews.
One or two dark shapes can be seen cutting ice,
singing as they reach down into a dishevelled
sea of transcendental homelessness.

Beached whales turn to shale in the underground
of potholes and cave-ins, a lava river
coursing through miles and miles of cracked tundra.
Hearts are being weighed in feathers.

'What do travellers do? They learn to walk
by leaning on their heads, like Lenz.
To step over difficulties by piling them up –
eskers, pingos, drumlins, abruptly calving glaciers.'

Far away, we hear the tribulation of a million diatoms,
foraminifera waving goodbye. 'Where now?
Sunlight's a burden on our backs.
All our conversation gets sucked up the flue.'

So we burn each other's skin like strange attractors,
rush-light salmon leaping in the slop-bucket
like our hearts did the day we stood
and cheered an iceberg's slow carriage to the equator.

Muir's Horses

So the comets finally make it to the sea.
Another hoof is melting in the heat.
So many blades are opening swart flanks.
Hippolytus dies, and Artemis shrugs it off.

A tragic chorus tries to bite its nails.
Christ knows why God has left him cold.
So many stories have no way to end.
So many stories cannot count.

Pain is a star that we can touch in trouble.
It tells us nothing, and it gets it right.
The way a horse is tortured in the gym.
The hundredweight hindquarters in the air.

We notice now the wretched space
once called a story is a press of flesh.
Another table upturns in the mud.
Comets are made of carbon and iridium.

My Friends and the Mountain

for A.G. and K.J.

They set out before daybreak, heretics
who'd never again settle for Cain and Abel
sermons on wet Sundays, not for the airy
resolve of an epic with little more to recommend
      than drop-scapes

where climbers owlishly get up for a piss
in the stony moonlight, base-camp
silhouetted in a landscape as transparently inner
as outer, smallish figures aloof and breathing
      isolate

office numbers. Back home
hops and malt were the usual social glue – commonsense
and an assembly of non-practitioners
settling against the bleak toehold purities
      of minds bound

elsewhere, to what is lethal and alone
and finds itself dragged bodily up the chain of being,
its amounting-to-nothing. I lost both
my friends, though they came back from the mountains
      long ago,

from the cliffs of fall, trading terms with the beast
and then the Buddha. (I'd gone to live
where Rilke wrote about the pure denial of summits.
Near enough the edge, I stubbed my toe
      on bedrock

and still didn't see it, that last homestead.)
Meltwater went sheer, deaf to its own intent.
Days on days made years. What they found was one high
nakedness, body heat: the godhead
      rapt and gone.

Zoo News

'When you've gone down under, come back up.'
So much was zoo news, for an evening.
Then you idled down a quiet street, in mild air,

to press your hands on the cooling mass,
and looked out, from as far inside. Someone would
whistle by and give you a lesson in life.

'Breathe, count your chickens, and don't drop
any more clangers in the Company's pound.
A place so featureless you'd think it extravagant.

Either way, it's where you get to cut ice
in a swelter of surgical-green citrus plantations,
all of Rainbow Snake's names for the day.'

Deep in the desert, the evangelist of barking shins
was just a boy with a box of matches.
Someone like you, in a tuft of eagle feathers.

'Brother, you can swing the light how you want.
Its map of thunder, scalds and grub caresses
holds little splinter nodes of promise.'

So a town looked up, loaded and preposterous;
hostage to bright air, chest-deep swimmers
and the rubber manacles of the constables in blue.

And how the right-side-up wanted the sun!
Clouds were cattle. People huddled on the hill
talking to each other, a suddenness of miles

and light in shoals and the names still burning.
Nightfall, shortfall: Castor and Pollux were up
nuzzling their manes in Berenice's Hair.

Voices from the street were almost gone.
Brilliantly sharp, zoo would make its own way home.
'Now you've gone down under, come back up.'

Love and Logic

Why now if not at all
next to the proof of need
which never is or cannot come?

It never seems as if
approximations of the why
will start to go until.

Logic has lost its way,
one arm disarmed,
the other dealing out its hand.

Intelligible last horizon,
the land is dark.
The days are yes and no.

After a time is after all.
No need to offer words unless
their loss of it explains.

Things

Life and Spirit spoke together
about the firebird's fabulous return.
Things are hard, things lay us bare

against the mirror, in the register
of white and inner places, out of harm.
Life and Spirit spoke together,

loving the way the streets are whirr
and drone, and floating on alarm.
Things are hard, things lay us bare

between the dreams of rush hour
and exhaust, the way our bodies burn.
Life and Spirit spoke together

of a bird collided with a star.
Now we know why years confirm
things are hard, things lay us bare,

and stand and watch wheels chafe on tar,
the steaming vapours of the storm
Life and Spirit spoke together.
Things are hard, things lay us bare.

Between the Rhins and the Machars

1 *Beltane*
Beside the five-mile-long
lucent comb of the Scottish Riviera
I waited for the star-hunter
to tread across the bladderwracks
and stiff marram dunes
with his promise of boreal chases
and carnival half-truths.

Only begetter of widows and orphans!
Shoulderer of household insults!
Husk-of-a-signifier!

2 *Whirl the King*
His was the evangelical tongue of difference,
a whirl-footed tugger on the vernacular's apron-strings.

Son of Boreas – he stood up with Whirl the King
and sat down again, daunted by the entrails.

Then he leaned from his extravagant pulpit
to lambast the dunes: '*Steadfast, backsliders, steadfast*'.

Never a mender of faults or builder of level conversation,
I cursed his intransigence, giant slapper of faces.

3 *Sea Level*
Seagulls cried like rust, and a few rooks
tore from the high trees.

Listening above the steady griping
of the running blue conifers
I heard the Atlantic shelving and storing,
refusing to say whose fault it was.

4 *Casida*

Mother of all Our Sorrows,
guard of the living God and Christ's pains,
what is sunlight for, but to accuse us
having no burden on our backs?

5 *Radical Light*

What looked to me like justice
was the day-old congealed remains of comfort.

Conscience had no qualms whatsoever,
dozing off in the middle of a conversation
with a pumice stone as pillow,
lava that floats on the mind's surface.

6 *Leonine*

O Scotia Irredentia –

you stretch out a leonine
ampersand-long paw

and contemptuously flattened
the bickering ladders

of a fortified city,
the loudly disputatious

monkey grammarians who stood
insisting with their quills

the sea was a kind of desert.
(Industrious metaphor

for Black Douglas' black
heart to wander home upon,

driving the Gulf Stream
up the western seaboard

till it could go no further:
void now of its various booty

of areca nuts, plantains,
six-day-ripe pomegranates

and other frazeriana
from the Holy Land itself.)

7   *Tripes et Boyaux*
I dreamt an old northern whale-song
got logjammed in the contraflow
from Spitsbergen or Franz Josef Land –

a pumped-up bagpipe's keen
forecast of imminent disembowelment –
but it was only your hand guddling

through armour for a gravid yield of whelks:
ductile limpet-laboratories
with their viscera swilling round their feet.

8   *Claims*
Right outside our door, on the tidal sands,
the Solway was a long-running esturial commentary
on two nations shut down for the night.
It licked the delta's green iridescent stream
and hauled its sulphur dogs behind.
We'd go walking there, against the wind.

It offered us a wash of Windscale seahorses,
the give and take of fingerlands and shoals
and an oystercatcher winnowing out the difference
between the old-time charisma of ledgers.
The wind, glamorously, accelerated among stones
and the fickle geography of settlements.

22

9 Fugitive

A house we might have stayed in,
had it not been for the stars
and the cold hills,
the plummeting mercury
of my indecision,

the walk down the road
and the slattern roofs decking
a dandelion parade
that led us back, like weird news,
to life on myrrh mountain.

10 Charm

I've a charm for bruises,
I've a charm for naked faces,
I've a charm for odd diseases,
I've a charm for empty spaces.

So: if you want to, come.
If you don't, stay.
If you are to heal, heal.
If not, so be it.

★

Religion, Science, Politics

One of the hidden Babylonian versions of the Creation kept in the labyrinthine archives of the Endowment for the Humanities reads as follows.

In the beginning God created the blue cage and the slurry.

And the slurry was a plummet of emptiness, and there were no entranceways or exits in the dark deionized recesses, and the spirit was a primal quenching.

And God said, let there be fire-quick gourds and flowering wars, bright immensements so corrosive they obliterate all sameness, spectra and diffraction patterns, coincident breathings and slim icy toeholds on the bog of slurry. And there were integers and the next body. And God called the sieging Day, and the salvaging Night. And there was day, and night. That was the first.

And God saw it was not good and gathered it together in his palm like a shocked dove, and repented that He had made it, and kept it secret.

To which a reader in the early years of our century has annotated: This one must have wandered off before the names were taken back. And other, several decades later: Yes, and it was a refugee from the land called Goethe.

Empty Meeting Places

1

There's all the usual blather of the place.
Six members of the chosen church
among blunt grasses, burnishing a Haydn hymn
on a small green hill with a banyan tree.
>   Light shines on as many words
>   between the big white tent and the lamb
>   tethered to the peg.

2

And then as many groping lamely westwards
for the Jordan view, the late late sun
between log mills and muffled bungalows.
I'm the finicky boy with the smirk on my face.
>   Soon I'm asking what it means
>   to be standing in my Sunday best, coveting
>   the virgin daughters.

3

The glory vine climbs up the wailing wall
and the stars come down, strangely beckoning
rays on a flag wrapped round
our covenant with rich men in America.
>   Shakers of the thirteenth tribe,
>   this is Year One of the unredressable sixties'
>   Great Leap Forward!

4

Picture a fire-engine dousing the hall,
wives with hats on, massed ranks
agape at the Malibu doctrine – shake it out
for Hobbes' hydraulic whale.
>   What does the sole survivor say,
>   broken hearted on the Staten Island ferry?
>   'Brethren, Beloved Brethren.'

5

What I see now is my mother and father's
damp faces, rapid northern salaams
to lift them out of range, not leave them here
high in the sky and nobody at home.
> They sing of heave and hinder
> voices rising above the standing maize,
> the furniture unmoved.

6

So here we are at the end of things,
the swallow's tail in a separate dispensation;
laughter at the sight of us
squeezing through the narrow gate.
> Of the amazing conversions
> what's left are empty meeting places,
> hunger and too much.

Westward Sailing Dissenters

Man is a wolf to man. They fed us on that millenarian maxim
            till the cows came home
and the ice-breaking cry of infants announced a new harvesting
            of souls, membranous

sacs of being lifted clean from their slither and slop. Deeper
            down in a bog of burdens
iron gouged the loam, farming more than the furrows in our brow;
            umpteen dragon-toothed

reasons why the past would get us too, with its big blue Zephyrs.
            Reason spat on the ground
quoting the bit about violence in heaven, and didn't have to close
            our eyes, a mission gone

berserk, unable to restrain its westward sailing dissenters.
            Hard spires, wooden roofs:
Calvinia held out against TV and the loosely insinuating ionosphere
            in all the time it took

a sweat-stained hat to be raised for the passage of a woman, one
            of Zion's daughters
taking a leisurely perusal of the window of the hardware store.
            It was a lovely way to walk,

to raise agony-aunt hackles, to make the weather flash outside the
            door as if we weren't descendants
of the folk who'd farmed the velvet country, on the Appalachian
            slopes; when we danced there, poorer

than we knew, history rubbed off our names, and didn't much care
            if we ever came back
(it was late in the day), siphoning fish-octane to make it home
            to the edge of harm, settled

as anyone ever could be, watching how thoughts swarm indifferently
            over meadows and gullies.
And this is the field-guide they left, full of the hundred-and-one things
            asked for by the agents,

murder-your-brother types from the city where they must have heard
        talk of the far-sighted
fervent preachers who saw God's hand in every pie, but wanted it all
        squashed level flat

as the bruised stubble fields. Swallows sagged in the smashed light
        and it was as much hope
and hurt as a sermon could bear. It had been a long time since anyone
        startled at the whirr

of grasshoppers, slow scrub fires starting from one cloudy perception
        and passing beyond all
understanding. Only pigs looked close at the dreary prairie winds
        and the hunkering pit

heaving with spawn, summer's return among the pokeweed's scrubby
        disentitlements of tundra.
Some winters, though, there'd be utter stillness and a fog-bound
        grievousness, perfunctory

double-backings of the beast, yells not daring the name, days
        they might have thought
this land was truly glutted in its gloom. For a moment up north
        hope was a hesitation

as, one by one, they tried to drum up courage to cross the bar. Perhaps
        There'd still be amazement
buried in the hills, fool's-gold, Indian tales of coyote in the know
        tucked under the topsoil,

recitations of all that wishful thinking to keep families intact, long
        after the burning books;
cardinals and dogwood, silence talking to itself under spruces
        as day falls to its doom

and thought is nothing more than a congregation dispersing
        after the watery Baptist
bracelets, faces kind and unweighted. Then talk of the town,
        talk of a good man gone.

A Glory Hole

Things ripen, and fall open.
Ezekiel's locusts have their work cut out
among sassafras and dogwood.

Ants find small comfort
in a baptist hall conflagration.
I can barely peer out through the blaze,

perched in one of the faultlines
of the porous Rock of Ages.
Even so, I'm trying hard not to look

askance, bagging so many dry souls
in a lochan by the Jordan.
This strict unreasonable people

gives me two clues to climb on:
either your heart gets hardened in the fire
or the Lord pours it out, once.

The Man William

He came with a switch in his hand
and said the white hot burning was the sun.

Something to be ploughed back
remorselessly, hard into the harrows

with only a fork of hazel –
Albion's tiller or Milton's moral wood –

to guide him between the high hills
and the hollows, stumbling

rebuffed into a reality not his own
(and not mine either) –

a landscape with its single ruined bothy,
bare plank of some bare ship

and a fire in its flank
to char the core, the way it breaks

when the waves fold behind it...
There's no refuting his deliberate hand

now, only a tree without leaves
and a gullible blanket of frost on the fields

where night has already fallen
and nothing goes, except without saying.

A Whale Full of Believers

1

One final day's amassing bulk
waits for the sign in a warm front room;
at-swim, all-whale. Some hurt
has emptied out its guts;
and the curtains billow open like sails,
unswingable and getting damp,
not catching happiness.

2

The watching wondering find their voice
no matter where, no matter how.
What Jonah did at sea
is jubilee, pent like the land:
warm hearth to ridge, the hope of feet
is soon to lift from mud.
Hosannah in the highest, fish.

3

A whale is all one mouth that spouts
coordinates for cutting loose.
From x to y to z,
Leviathan is where amassers chafe,
vehicle of what large earth
wants back, and keeps on taking –
lagged, the living rock.

Numbers

In Genesis, wombs are honey pots that open and close without the least embarrassment or hindrance. One twin sticks his hand through the dilated cervix and the midwife ties a scarlet thread to his wrist, saying 'this one came out first'. Thinking he's been perhaps too hasty, he pulls back his hand and his brother falls into the breach. But he's still the firstborn by virtue of the scarlet thread.

The listing of names itself becomes the story. When I was a boy I had to sit through long triumphant recitations of names from the first books of the Bible: Genesis 5 or 10 for example. 'And to Shem – to him also were sons born; he is the father of all the sons of Eber, the brother of Japheth the elder. The sons of Shem: Elam, and Asshur, and Arphaxad, and Lud, and Aram. And the sons of Aram: Uz, and Hul, and Gether, and Mash...'

In no time at all, and even after the exodus from Egypt there are 601,730 people in the Numbers census.

Clearly there is some hydraulics in all this: the sheer weight of ancestors exerts an irresistible downwards traction on the musculature of the womb and expels the child, so that if we can agree that body and belief are essentially the same, then the womb is a receptacle with not just the standard function of continence but also to hide one thing from the other.

'I will multiply your descendants as the stars of heaven and as the sand which is on the seashore.' It's hard to imagine one of the sons of Israel on a rough country track walking out of the desert. Perhaps he was looking for Rebecca to pour him some water for his camels. He would dig, if she held the jug. Perhaps, biting into a pomegranate, she thought he was being a bit literalminded.

Their families would have rescued them, but these were the first days of the nation and there was stacks of work to be getting on with.

The Fever Hospital

1

Jean (soon to be) Singer walks down the road from the fever hospital,
nurse's uniform in her bag, smitten by a man called Nelson
whose throat trembles as he sings of six nuptial eggs in an apron
and a woman whose skin is alabaster, lily-of-the-valley.

2

On the day she married they gave her a po filled with salt,
symbol of seedcake and propitiousness, the sweat-shop
in the diminishing bedroom made distant with tea ceremonies,
weedy mother-of-pearl and several dolphins drowned in porcelain.

3

Even combing her hair in the washbasin carried a religious charge.
She hadn't forgotten the day she'd picked skin off the man
with scarlet fever, a rubber sheet for the administration of unguent.
Was she a believer? Justice, she shyly insisted, was just ice.

4

That was her unflappable feeling for our dubious mountain talk,
grandpa's address from a soap-box to the woolpack clouds.
When the strain of being cheerful started to show, she turned finical,
telling her son in Australia she was a captive audience – native and
     naive.

5

I think she hoped the stones would grow like coral, gloopy Red Sea
     lichen
flame and growl across the garden to kindle leaves on the compost.
Looking at her life, she must have thought her head for heights
was what sparrows sang of, their precise feeling for the gable end.

6

I started to tell her about Orwell's stay in the same contagious hospital
but the story came out mottled and lichenified, a smear of zinc.
She was afraid she'd never put her finger again on the scripture she
    liked best
about myrrh and henna, and a man passing the night between her
    breasts.

7

Somewhere there were peace and tranquillisers for her, mundane
    eggs.
Only that day she stripped the wallpaper and assaulted the book
and breezily, haphazardly began to throw chintz out of an upstairs
    window –
bedpan first, and then all the white-glazed nenuphars of Nineveh.

8

Which just goes to show I'm not to be trusted with dead relatives, glaciers,
storms in teacups and other paraphernalia of the resurrection fever
since fevers abate, and tranquillisers work, and even grandpa had a cameo
    role
in the great musical stirring that came one Sunday to Auldhouse Park.

Boy

1 House of Shaws
Before I darkened the door, I tried out different versions.
Strange how the days are a perfect fit, how the enigmatic ladder
takes me up to Uncle Ebenezer's attic, like prissy David Balfour...
Strange how the soul creeps up the tongue's thick fur, and gags on air
and we're all helpless at the end, historians of harm.

Nothing less strange than my mother shaking out the tablecloth
and intimacy being folded. Time to put out the light   .
on Earl Grey. Days freak up the trees. Home is where the heart hides.

2 Song of Songs
There were stars and everything inside the pleats of plaid.
I held her twine cat's-cradle-wise and watched my mother ball the
     wool
to make a ladder with her pins. That would be my scala enigmatica
lifting me up out of soggy Scotland to breathe fire and violins
above the ranks of the squeaky, responsible dead.

Everything was fresh in the small rooms of the Bridegroom.
I would sing unto Jehovah as long as I liked. First I would look my
     father
in the eye, up the ladder as he painted, telling me cock and bull.

3 Living with the Micmac Indians
Boy laid the table, heat left the hills, and nothing was said.
It was a good opener, but I doubted it would carry me across the Clyde
to America, where ladders dangled invitingly for all believers.
I told my mother the future was stirring beneath us
and she wouldn't have it. She gave me notice, like a tiny star.

On a clear day the view was Ailsa Craig, and all the way to Spain,
and it was only a question of time before a trapdoor opened in the sky
and I could see how far the world had come, and my childhood.

4 The Pandemonium Model
I liked the bit about Darwin standing on Aristotle's shoulders.
In the pandemonium model, string made a ring, subset induced a forest
and boy sat watching rain falling where the window was.
Even the clouds were an impossible colour, and the journey was longer
and more perilous than anyone had thought, whispering, being loyal.

First Man stood on the eastern side of the World of Blue Haze
and planted the pumpkin, the canteloupe, the water- and the muskmelon.
It was about coming alive again, without ladders, without snakes.

5 A Scene from the Battle of Lepanto
So it seemed we were scampering up the same bars and lozenges
looking for the stick that crossed rivers on its own, repetitive pug-
    angels
and choral threnodies, B-roads not leading anywhere in particular
    except up.
That year I was clinging to a balsa spar from the battle of Lepanto
and first home as always, declaiming odes to my socks.

But the Biblical idiom stayed, the fat ram in the thicket, the gob words.
Now it seemed no embarrassment to be unladdered, to achieve exact
    notation
of what was always quiet in the house, what the wind couldn't shift.

6 The Amazing Dreamcoat Version
In the last version, I put on my coat of three colours (hope, sex and
    dogma)
that might almost have been any colour, the way things were going,
my era sliding down like a rusty pram into the Cart and Kelvin.
I was small, and waiting for the world to start while Glasgow fell to
    bits
and my mother pummelled my hair dry and sleep dried like salt.

There had to be an end to knowing things, their stony aggrandisement,
if only it might be what my mother taught me of conscience and
    charisma,
the light-fluked scald of sun on scales, swimming horizontal music.

7 *Sitting it out between Orc and Urizen*

Other scenes from my visionary childhood between Blake and Bunyan
are not for public consumption, and certainly not those cosy figures
running up the Alexandria Parade, hats spontaneously igniting
in defiance of the calendar's forecast: rain from the west.
Boy was seen throwing buns in the Apollo and Flora tea gardens.

Sometimes there were mild answers when they rang on the door.
Sometimes there was a sense of the impending blue sky.
Sometimes I remembered the look of my mother's liberation
    theology.

8 *The Divine Esther*

What was left to do, believers, but let the snake swallow the egg?
I enjoined it with my several versions, with Stevenson's rickety stairs,
trams, rope-tricks, the home left behind, irritable bowel syndrome
and beauty queens called Esther in the eastern provinces.
(Snakes don't climb ladders, so we abandon them to the obvious.)

This was the weird mission of our Bible readings: to domesticate
curved space and endorphins and the decay of heavy water
with David Balfour's quick lurch into difference, his place in space.

★

Don't Stop Here

I set out, believing in the redemptive power of work, and went over the world's edge for my sins, and wouldn't stay put, out of my mind for lack of sleep, for raising too many eyebrows and too few rafters above the Plimsoll line,

And went on a windy road that wouldn't give, not even after admiring the fig trees and banana plants in any of a hundred country places, backpack clanking with pots and pans and Mother Courage's feel for the one-armed bandit in the shop beyond the pepper signpost,

And went to the moon on a pumpkin seed, language unravelling in my hand and time like a hint of resilience on the upper lip while the sun, that scarab on a stalk, was all my allure,

And went beyond the mountains and other impediments, cactus-succour and calories in the boot, heading for the mystical gutta-percha cricket of places where the one truly sacred fetish was a black box and where I hoped they'd invite me in, beyond our obvious differences, small towns dressed for dreaming, horses racing on sand,

And went into the lightly-peopled interior, startled not to see anywhere about me the cough and chaos of city-streets, traffic, hammer reds and abdicating greens, the talking dollar disappearing from view into concrete's Mayan stillness.

I set out, hero to one, and knocked over the landscape.

A Clear Thought

In between the yellow utes
and the flame-tree garageways,
my wife at the wheel –

upward to the scorched mesas
and camel-track droppings
of overland Australia;

weatherboard houses reconciling
to the desert's boiler room,
sad suburbs without a centre,

figures agape, wondering what
on earth. Two transients,
we were crossing a language

bigger than its markers, burning
rubber, clambering up
the loose gravel of our talk –

baskers on a broad hammock
slung between gum-trees, the Hill
below, revealing its workings –

row upon row of indigo
gardens, helium and the honey-tree;
desire like a flowering aquifer.

The Pinnacles

These are the Pinnacles,
an austral sublime
safe behind breeze-block
and a zigzag of towers
on the bulldozers' way
to the refuse tip.

Dream hard and you,
dear Lotto winner, might see
last night's sinners
float across the Zinc Lakes,
one strapped to the spars
of the Pioneer century,

both ears greased
against the siren-sound
of a hero getting his own way
while the wife brushes off
spinifex in very sight
of these odd lunar droppings.

Fuse Wire

Two miners out there in conversation, hugging a sealed road so straight it hurts the eye. Each has a message for you, which he transmits with a rare smile:

'Pack every seam with ore.'
'Let it breathe!'

What you have to do is this.

Drill down into the massed ranks of quartz: geodes, orts, outer integument of the first-time-hypothesized bones or roots flung up out of their heat-sink (impacted for now, but only in English's down-to-earth, all patents pending). Tamp it deep into the windpipes of swallowholes and graben.

Hold your breath, and a pouchy thought-song lifts off into the outer dimension of air, a peer-reviewed evolutionary QA/QC update, hosannah of the Big Bang. One of several thousand inhabitants between breakfast music and the ductile hills might have heard something, but it would have gone unremarked – a door slamming in the wind, an echo calling back a name.

Then you can smell it, a fish-oil foetor signalling time's regain of the air, hard things glittering in the air, fault-line seedings, dry residues left in a crucible to bring down rain.

And that's the escape route you'll worry into: an earth scientist's pet theory of the combustible spirit, bluer than its elements.

Shorts

1

A swift January no-no
to the lame fossicker hope
of Merely Surviving –
about as realistic as swimming
up the Birdsville Track.

2

We stocked up on antiveneme
for the desert poisons
trod on under blowsy mulgas
busily tapping us
for a serpentine omen of water.

3

A deep soil contour-map
trumpeted the unclaimed follicles
of the emu oestrus cycle
freshly painted on
the ammoniacal municipal loo.

4

Rain thunders east
with the Indian Pacific railroad
to Woop Woop's
screeds of Mitchell grass
and baked bean earth.

5

Squatter real estate
sprouting on the edge of town
duly bears the exquisite graffito:
'Come on out, white fella,
this town is surrounded.'

6

An outbreak of plague locust dreaming
was reported to have occurred
between the Bible Hall
and the Barrier Miners' Association's
cordon of pigmy palms.

7

A crumpled saltbush haze –
one flat terrible glare
where nothing human stays upright
and what does is ultimate
starch, termite cool.

8

In the TV ghetto
what happens behind walls
is some kind of curdled death,
pain being an alien
approachable only by stealth.

9

New settlers like us
go in willful pig-ignorance
of the named stones
and shadow-decked slabs
hiding so many dead hunchbacks.

10

It's easy to learn the bush trick
of annulling the occasional
turbulent desert storm
by simply going outside, busy
at a snail's pace, and staring.

Sham Umbrellas

Hardly anyone these days
might credit the small instances
sustaining dry scrub, liquidities of bush.

These people do, pursuing their purpose
into huge rain, the processional
dream-journey hushing through the room

to a gathering around a glass.
Thirst is a night-blooming invocation
tagged to the tree of stories.

Swimming on Dry Land

Even after they'd dropped out of view,
those first Scots Australians, they could still be heard:
a long-lunged howl from under battens
and the waterline. They'd never heard tell of mangroves
tapping for salt water, of sand-storms
and clay scalds: the erosive knowledge that attends
making ends meet when ends can't meet.

Half the family would be dead
before they glimpsed the great Australian desert's
half-sea, down on down, in the dark.
So much is obvious and quiet
and doesn't bear telling, like the crawl
of those who went deeper into the earth's room,
begging the ground not to hurt them.

Gob Road

Imagine the earth's own shape,
a deep pit for hiding hurt –
and ask where the gob road goes,
black kings; ask who dared draw breath
in expensive light, then said:
two steps forward, one step back.

What are words for? Talking shop
and sleeping on, good luck tales
of lag faults, gouge zones, scour lakes;
kindly stars of lode brought home
like a yes: little ice age
of junk and seepings and land

slips, things the tongue gets caught on
walking back up the gob road.
(Even black kings feel the heat
kilometres underground.)
Life is a hole plugged with love
and lumber, buckets of it.

The Cages

As like as not

        there'd be a long row:

each dressed in his black

        work suit,

mark of the Cyclops

        on his gradual brow,

lunch in a casket

        belted to his waist,

swinging, swinging

        the hypothetical bird –

every last one

        as trench-quiet

as the outward bound,

        each holding a token

from the broken hill.

        Feldspar and oxides

sprout in their hands,

        a rust of utensils

at the approachable rockface

        beggars belief:

big green envy

        of living in the light.

We watched them go down

        and come back up,

giants perforating

        earth-time

into our flat cries,

        night after night

unburdening their backs

        of lag and load.

A Hole in the World

At Broken Hill you were defeated
W.H. Auden

Hole would be there, staring me out,
hauling a hard look down
past slag heaps and coke ovens –
a gash in the longwall face
and brooding empty barrows, so much
dark in the shifts of light.

And there it was, plumbing
the earth's cracked crust, starry-eyed.
Silence was so much damp breath
hugging the surge tanks, sun
and slow change, all the massed
dazzlements of carbon.

Fear of it, my slabby medium.
I wrestled with strange
news, on the brink of understanding
why a city wouldn't work.
All the echo said was pledged;
a licence lost, less said.

Knowledge had nothing left to do
but kick away the baffles.
There was a rush of air, a resettling
in that hole in the world;
everything, from the Creation onwards,
clear as day, except the flaw.

The Water Tower

Wonder at it –
the ruined water-tower,
its cool fuselage
like a prophet in the scrub,

a rain-revivalist
waiting all day
for a hectoring vision
of sand, wind and stars,

that slight involuntary
creaking of the skin,
the metal flanges
sagging into rust, rungs

of a Jacob's ladder
slung against the sun's
hot echoings.
All night it groans

like nothing else on earth,
a hardskin silence
calling up a cargo-cult
for angels, moguls,

any kind of transiting
promoter. Look up,
it vaunts, at the vector-
shifts of satellites,

those lunar Hubbles
of the hopeful parched,
city-slickers
on the bitumen shores.

Dread relic, this
is the coming-full-circle,
one marrow's appeal
to the tabernacle choir:

it sings your asperities,
a reservoir on high
and the windows in a blaze.
Wonder at it –

the funnel of our faith
that lifts to rain,
pale citizen flakes
and the singing drowning.

Back, Brother, Back

To clear throats, Lake Anticipation and the all-at-sea
                    kaikuyu pastures,
tops of mornings, shade-seekers and the salt pans at Eyre,
to the Silver City Highway, demure sidewalks on stilts
                    for the next Great Flood
(though here won't be its first overswimming); to the lemon trees
at the back of the garden and weeks of extendible weather
                    living side by side
                    between the flimsy houses'

hydrant-draining 24-hours-a-day coolers; to the eczema sunsets
                    at Mundi Mundi
and a Gondwana seabed staging the nymph locust rain-dance.
To Nevertire, and a huddle of settlements called Eden;
                    green-ant directives,
light like iron, and January remodelling the steering wheel.
Believe me, Brother, Patterson's curse is something else again
                    and whatever you've read
                    the road to Gundagai

starts half a day ahead of here, well beyond the chatter
                    of Doug and Ruby
and the bougainvillea heaving mauve petals on the chook run.
To starting days: a baker, three hotels and the Peelers' pound,
                    foetal deep sleep
in the Two-Up palaces, Burke and Wills' calling-card at Wilcannia
where politically incorrect medicos lean across an interpreter's
                    middle-high Aranda;
                    To outcast economies

of spyglass kvatch and immemorial Brick Lane recitations;
                    to art for life's sake,
plein-ciel horizons, and the creek-bed wit of paperbark poets.
To redbacks in the toilet bowls, solar keratoses and wet beri-beri,
                    though in retrospect
and with our old friend the locust inspector coming for dinner,
we've hardly a worry, as the sociable swagger-idiom insists,
                    hanging up our laundry
                    of bush semaphore.

★

51

Up and Down the Ayr Road

for Gerald Mangan

Had you been up and down the Ayr Road once
or twice in a full moon,
you might have seen him too, a man with only
three things on his mind:

convoys of U-Haul juggernauts in front
that won't let him pass,
Covenanters on the shooting crests at Ballantrae
where Burns, at Shanks' pony's pace,

wrote back 'Life is all a VARIORUM', and Keats,
knee-deep in St John's-wort,
peered over the drop
and thought Ailsa Craig more 'omphalos' than Hellespont –

volcano stump of a glacial
slick that had shovelled topsoil south
from this granitic
anti-Greece. (There's probably a tourist-path

leading out across the schist and gneiss,
rich sea-tangs
of the ploughshare, exuberant clumps of lamb's lettuce
and the committed songs

of those who've looked over
Lear's shirt-tails, and seen the greenest grass
thriving on the plummet of the void.)
You might have seen him giving gas

to his hundred-horse-power, no doubt reflecting
he'd likely – more than not –
be clinging to a pencil when the seas go dry
and Scots clacks from one empty palate

to the next. So, as he skirts the potato fields
and creameries, bound this afternoon for the hill
flailing across the windscreen
and the giant hospital hull

where he'll be left to worry out
the social contract and its bad-faith Tory echo
masquerading as a *citizens'*
charter, open the window and you might hear Diderot

decanting 'Knowledge is Happiness' and believe it,
counting field after field of shy
dandelion-heads blown suddenly adrift
into another space

of seed-scatter vectors, effortless
upward soarings of chromosomes. Defoe the spy,
too, delimited these cloud-deft
gables, the spruce

herring-town anchors
interred inland, but didn't think it such a bind,
life that had reached one bend
in the road to Ayr.

A View of Luce Bay

for G, J and M

1

Look across the bay to where the Scares are waiting while we wear away. What do you see?

Thick mud bouillons; lacustrine herb gardens; wind-pummelled outhouses with cold grates; small silt harbours nobody but locals have access to; two-mile acreages, coal-burning vicinities blacker than underwater amethyst; wild garlic, mint and thyme pastures that hardly ever end in the kitchen.

An old potato culture, living better than ever at the heel-end of the twentieth century.

Oyster-catchers, dead myxo rabbits on the beach; the beach itself a long-drawn-out sigh trapping the mull's backwash with its stories of drowned liners and dispatches, apocryphal Armadas sealed in the merse, the Solway's rich alluvium.

Greens from emerald to lime; small-holds, villas, cringingly ugly box caravans behind stunted spruces.

2

Somehow, it's the remembered life: as if we had blown here like itinerant potato pickers with the August winds, sipping peatish rain as it slowly turns to whisky in a cooper's sump.

(One more station of the great Unheard-Of, Carlyle sitting at a gneiss table while he tracks the words *mankind* and *health* over four millennia. God the Father throws him an unwritten copy of *The Thirty-Nine Steps* to wedge with his foot against the draught, and still it's not clear who's imposing on whom.)

Or else, it's the wind's apostolic retort to the faint-of-heart, the Mediterranean household gods put in a discreet place with the bay leaves; thick animal smells drifting in the bay window left ajar at night, and announcing more rain tomorrow.

Herrings and shires, hopelessly partial proofs, truly remarkable things.

3

Awhirk, Ringuinea, Little Float: I carry the names in my pocket like charms.

Walking up gravelled approaches to their outhouses or unlatching doors into kitsch-haunted interiors, they salt me into their sense of place. In exchange, I gently advocate the art of self-criticism, orator to crazed mahogany boudoirs and asthmatic feathersprung beds with quicksand in their hearts.

Mostly they listen me out, and then range what I've said in a niche beyond their dignity.

But they keep tallies of dead relatives and how they went, and days when it didn't rain: theories of Scotland facing up to the future, conspicuous omissions of the country across the Solway, a native passion for the drama of sickness and health. Finally, they make no bones about what's irretrievably lost and what can be put right in the morning.

Coming back to the human condition and my businesslike angle on it, they tell me what I almost succeed in not remembering: there's cure, but none persuasive.

4

One house keeps drawing me back, a bivouac for moral mystics. In the front room, the only fittings are a bucket and a pile of felt blankets; there's almost nothing else aside from a shadow lying under the several layers and waiting for hope of better times.

Dirt under his nails, an old tin can and burner, a procession of ants leading to the flakes of shed skin. There's more to me than needfulness or neglect, he tells me, with a punch-line from Zapata, and an attitude from Beuys!

I can't help thinking of a man enduring the worse winter of his life daubed with tallow, and the survivalist humour that added a coat of goose feathers.

But then, he insists on the seventh visit, he's looking for lightness, unclutteredness, a new beginning. And he signals he going to stay put, sartorially squatting on his bone of Luz.

Which I try to understand, emptying my mind to enter his.

5

Going to work I notice the salt rime on the rhododendrons.

Inside: dossiers, sphygmomanometer, notepad, pens and mounds of government propaganda for the good life, a copy of *An Enquiry into Human Understanding* (some talking point!) and the profession's usual support material.

Patients, I suppose, might even get used to my talking voice, as it lingers at the tuberous knots and resins, time like a helium balloon escaping out the skylight window, or those long pauses where I can't think what comes afterwards and console myself by saying it out loud: better not force it.

The recondite logic of things raises its fur to peremptory newcomers, and cannot be cajoled.

Our trial by co-existence, I called it once, hoping people would understand my openness to process too.

6

Despite the man-hours and Chekhov's journey to Sakhalin, silence keeps falling on desolate uniform voices, on Unhappiness dying to be loved, and getting hitched to Habit.

Sometimes it's critical, a theorem of empty spaces hunching over itself for the duration, moist with meaning as spindrift blows off the swell and salt radicals line up on the beach like redcoats, bayonets fixed to extirpate exotica flourishing along the Scottish Riviera, ghost-gums and cacti and squat etiolated palms.

Naked, zealous, it walks straight out of gladness into the thick plate glass called disaffection. All I do is bathe it in opinion, sliding my hand into every scapegrace wound, understanding what's required, just a word out loud.

Among the smell of chlorhexidine and benefit forms I chew on Thoreau's 'there is something of the burlesque about the Truly Earnest Man'.

Silence falls on us, sitting in a white room.

7

All this self-sufficiency; it's making me edgy – I've grown too soft in cities, too tainted by the will.

Language lived here till it became fushionless and mouldy, was leapt over at fords, laid down like stones in a gullion; local burrs, fern, hirsts and tummocks, intelligence brushing the hand in the neapish silences of winter.

It wasn't too difficult to imagine someone had come round one day, someone with substance in the community, and planted a pole with the legend KEEP OUT.

8

An old farmer sits in the kitchen, boots off, with a skinned rabbit for company. Outside, a huddle of Friesians stands in its steam and stares downwind. The shakes he has are Parkinsonian, intent on making him ponder spilt milk, unpasteurised, I speculate, and from the herd. Six copper pots hang from the scullery wall and an old pre-war mangle serves as clothes' horse.

Before long we're sharing a tarry cup of tea and he's showing me where he got struck by shrapnel. 'So how did you get to be this old?' I ask him, meaning ninety. 'Simple, son, I just keep on breathing', breathed on me like a benediction.

9

This afternoon there are cows on the road. There's nothing for it, but to wait till the poleslung bladders make it back through the mud, swaying like quinquiremes as they nudge the car, huge swollen lackadaisical lumberings, mounting each other in train.

One peers in through the floating windscreen but it defies her: tall creamery stacks and washing swim away along the blank ribbon roads.

On these back roads, it's all ordnance survey. The accomplished view of Ireland over High Spittal and rain falling on the Machars coming down from Whirlpool; everything damp and speculative, the Scottish sublime a detour down the byways of obsolete usage, sheepdrove paths and cowtrails and one-shop towns before the great salt sweep of the Luce cuts its swaithe, Latinity's edge, light trembling in tin buckets and people waiting for their boat to come.

10

In the car I screen what look like applications for mercy stifled by a deconstructionist from the DSS. Morphine, morphemes; spouses who've never talked it out, the old Tolstoyan fear impaled on the window frame. What's said, what's left unsaid; what escapes down the lemming lanes, tapeworm loops of the devil's mind. Lines of connection blow like spittle in the wind.

Coming down to the half-moon of the bay, the bombing range and the marshy breeding grounds of transiting battalions, I watch what happens when the sun ventures out.

Cars line up on the coast and cups of tea get served. Folk I've probably sounded stare oceanwards out of their lives, forgetting what brings them here, to the edge of things, the sea droning like a domestic epic that's drunk and smashing its crockery on the rocks, all glug and peristalsis.

A briny sink shifts with platitudes and affectionate asides, the watchers staying till they're sure they've seen it once – the brief plume of a porpoise out at sea. Or they don't, and return home, the rain in sheets and the sea full of salt.

Doing Calls on the Old Portpatrick Road

1 *Seven Kingdoms*

Towns, settlements, two acre allotments
and humpbacked hills that might
or might not be something else;

figures you made out once from the door
ducking as they walk beneath low
swooping shoals of birds, flask-finders

bound for dunes and bomb sites
and the quarry's inverted hill of beans;
three-hundred year old Gaelic elocutionary

lessons – Airyligg, Balquhidder –
and the foot-dragging spoor of rain;
black polythene-wrapped silage bales

and fields with fleece in the wires
cambering from barely visible Ireland
on one side, to Man on the other,

three of the seven kingdoms looked out to
from the lighthouse, on good days –
a neuk then, sleeved with its bellibuchts

and puddled with gorrochs, shingle
all along the western bay road
falling over itself to praise the view

once explained to an observant tourist.

2 Gut Bucket

I watched him sluicing out a bucket full of brilliant fish,
his hands sleek fish themselves.
                              He took me in and put me down
in sight of the sea and the turf's smouldering relics
while he stood greeting like a man who'd seen too much
of primaeval oceans, the earth's wide lap or a few slippery stars
scorched on the carpet. It was enough to empty his cargo
in the coal shuttle. Then he smiled, to put me at ease.

Having found the bucket still steaming in the snow
I closed the yard gates and walked back up the gravel path,
leaving with the thing I'd borrowed from his life,
its dull weight no use at all, like a whelky boathook lured
from the seabed.
                    I tramped away again, straining to remember
what he'd said. Day was behind my shoulder. Austerity
would tare our implements, bucket stay bucket.

3 MacCaig's Field

Today was only a little storm.
But you cleared chairs for it, sheltering
between the fall of Troy
and the nation buried in the loam.

The human dimension was a barricade
around such serious wrecks;
Terminus' thunder-stone, words in the field
for the man you thought you were.

You waited regardless, leaning
on a signpost, rained-on and historical;
ground observer in the field
that was only a little field.

When I brought up that subject again
they all looked at me as if it were hanging from my nose,
the meaning of why we grow and turn to rubble.
They watched me like some exotic animal
with a few words to my name, and not even those I'd grown up with.
I watched them back, and pocketed their silences:
people with toast, people with aprons, people with hopes
of good days and the best not yet come.

Only my wife fully grasped my abscondment.
Here was temptation, and other wives swimming through hills
and all the silence that a man might need.
I passed them in the morning, the mantle cooling,
and watched a mirror grip the lochan,
. tiny straw cities flourishing along the burns.
Poised daytime observers, they hid their symptoms under stones
and figured me out as an urban guerilla.

It seemed like a war zone, gorse-fires flickering on the hills,
heaps of devotion everywhere,
eggs in miners' knees, air hunger, a Crusoe syndrome;
though all I could see was a red tractor dragging gulls behind it.
When we talked, they looked over my shoulder
for the horizon to run aground, and waited to be amazed;
total strangers to the facts,
their late desert flowering dumbness.

Radio asked for silence, to go back to the start.
One patient said an angel crossed the room that day.
I was down reading racks of spines,
tapping the floorboards, going from room to empty room.
Now and again I heard an accent plead with the wall
and drive away forever to the city.
Reality was a body stroked for its complicity.
Later a few stars came down to the edge of the field.

5 The Way It Works

The way it works is: A
tells B the story – his story
in his words – and B tells
A not to cheat on particulars.

And when B is through
he holds the meaning up to A,
carefully averting his eyes
from the Gorgon's head

perched between them on the table
or leaning from a shelf.
At which point A is able to enjoy
the benefit of the doubt

and both fuse in a hot instant
since the revelation is also a proof.

6 Scant Resources

Not knowing how to comfort her
I held her wiry hand
and told her about the camphor-hunters
pushing through the hemp,
pairs of wagtails that each morning
hexed me when I gained the car.

Rescue from this old folks' home
was out of the question.
Her jaws worked, stunned beyond belief
at the same old hump of hills,
the always-on TV, a day-glo flicker
almost bigger than the window.

Some were out hunting their deaths.
Pain was something she'd dug from the Book.
It was busily being metamorphosed
into mineral seams and faults.
Who'd expect a witchetty grub totem
standing in a field of maize?

One day, we all go too deep
into ourselves, despite the counsel
of the hoary medicine-man
and our hapless mothers, beseeching us.
We go into the thick night
and then the only landscape, older than us.

The camphor-hunters were smoking out a hive.
I touched underwater tree-taps,
strips of song on the upper branches,
years ruffling the surface
of a life as it slowly lapsed into the sump,
bitter, defiant, its bed on its back.

7   *Plover Eggs in a Field of Pumpkins*

Error was something perfected –
that was where I was living.
An edifice for lying low in.

People had their trusted stony truths,
bruised, not quite habitable.
The other, abruptly virulent kinds

were passed on like flu
by addressing the sleeve, gently,
of a gape-mouthed utterer.

8   *Critical Theory*

Everything she does with her body suggests
I won't escape with a word in passing.

So I watch her sit down in the chair
and close the door on rusty usages,

habits and habitats, views of Atlantis
in the ruffled pond called chagrin.

63

Whatever you say just isn't subtle enough
to make a distinction between truth

in its moley burrow, and a figure
naked, running the gauntlet among clothed

arbiters of opinion. How like yourself, I think
and vent my annoyance in the small

interstices where burdens become balloons.
Why do you call it failure now my heart breaks?

9   Enemy of the People

Looked at one way, I was the village explainer
shovelling sun and moon

into an open ditch, leaving them in the dark
totemic ferment of a provincial

afternoon, most of all the ones in the corner mouthing
that'll bloody well learn you –

agog at the hard facts, last of a lost tribe
like the Shuswap or Coeur d'Alêne

exempt from the pub due to my overingenious
readings of their body fluids.

I know, I know: nobody buys it, this poem
for those who don't read poems, as it were free

of every obligation except the need to dream up
another: here's a man you can't lean on.

Worse than doctor's platitudes
are those raised structures
worked on relentlessly,

superb vantage points
between the shooting ranges
strung out on pheasant pastures

where you might observe
pain standing in the clearing,
a dim daze of mist

and the creak of oars;
positions false in themselves
and besides, not for usage.

Someone's worked the ground before
and now it's exhausted –
pebbled, thistled, nitrogenous:

years dispersing at that utterly
alien place, the body;
seed-storms and night-sight

and the gift of tongues
in one ear and out of the other,
sleek as Minerva's owl

but recognising (just about) where
it gets off, people
still making ends meet.

11 *A Shining*

It was tenure in the wilderness at High Mark farm,
up-country marshes, fens, bracken, sheep stomps.

> I went there to give bad news
> and watch what they'd do with it.

Like that time the family stopped at the road's edge
and something still breathed in the wreckage.

> Silence fluttered across the room
> like a sparrow among the high rafters.

They'd already worked out the terse coded message
darkening the door of the hay-bound paddock.

> Somehow I'd trampled on their eggs
> and cut a furrow across the carpet.

I listened to my own voice, a damp dishcloth
squeezed out on whatever might have been shining.

> Better gobsmacked by hard rain, one said,
> than the horse doctor of happenstance.

12 *Graham's Landing*

> *'The ear says more
> Than any tongue'*

I thought I spoke your language
asking what the matter was, the wrong.
I only wanted to know your history
framed in the window of our time.

Which of us should have had first say?
One who inhaled the long firth,
one who seemed a slow-island-Joe,
one who clambered the bare scree up –

The house put on its afternoon disguise,
wrong way round and inside out.
Language was an unreliable hidey-hole
for two social beasts in harness:

me, losing track of the unreliable words
called bait and purchase, you
dangling them in the cold blue sound
that wandered past the window.

13 Ancient Radio Dream

I
What could Radio Atlantis tell of deep sea monsters,
of the Ark at flood-tide and a pigeon's post;
of a few unassuming faces at the edge of their own language,
down on all fours, listening to the grass bleat?

Work, don't despair, they'd say, we're a companionable lot;
and then play dumb while the fields cooled under the stars.
Radio Atlantis was a wind machine, a lapsed curious way
for time to be ductile, for the boat to take them there, over the horizon.

II
The wind was blowing the day after the Flood,
so someone must have spoken after all
like a leaky bath, or a puddleful of memory
quivering on land, in the wet west.

I dreamed of stippled gouge marks,
advertisements of feral passage, leaf-talk and owls;
no door to doom, just the tramp of rain
and little weed-clumps history might have overlooked.

Their land of cumulus was all geology
and the radio was calling, calling that the boat was ready
and they should now intone please
the words of the commandment, on the way to Paradise

star, stone, boat, leaf, rain, house, hair.

14 Bones and Feathers

Simply get up and go, striding
across the fields with your breath in front –
dog at heel, hobnails ringing on ridges –
and walk into the mountains, closing them behind

before your wife comes in with the eiderdown
and says for God's sake lie back and stop
making such an awful fuss.
Going, you take her most for granted,

since only the wind comes back from the hills
and whines beneath the doorstop,
buckets in a bind and pump handle frozen
and two oars on the roof like buckled femurs.

15 Two Minds

Not that you knew, but I came back on a hunch
screeching the gate open on the flagstones
and entering the dim cold kitchen,
coronation brasses gleaming in the gloom,
old newspapers damp on the floor and a scummed
residue in the cat's bowl. It was a week
too late to lift you upstairs off the candlewick,
chilled out of your wits.
                                    Like winter
or something more deeply dreaded, far in the mind,
I creep from house to house, barked at
till I reach the lace-curtained salty windows,
the inner hallows.
                              You'll be heaved aloft by adorers,
six mild men, and sealed with a hymn at Stoneykirk,
queen of the drones in a hive without honey.

16 A Small Exchange of Air

The door was open for air,
sudden escape, or his better half
eavesdropping next door.
I hope it won't take long, he said.

And I: William Osler, the places
you haven't been. Believe me,
there were another way
I'd rather discuss prize cheeses

wrapped in muslin, crop rotation,
spring roses breaking through
the hedgerows; even dirty
realism and non-biodegradables.

A pervasive sound swam
through the half-closed door.
A man and a woman were asking
who on God's earth I thought I was.

17 Spilt Milk

Inside, company made fresh tea
and I was invited to join.
To open the freshly baked bread
and taste the risen host.

It was understood the clock
stayed draped till her man had died.
He was trying, but his death
was lost in the woods,

a moonshiner or a card-sharp
who had other places to be
as he looked down on the demesne.
Wasn't this the day marked out

by friends and neighbours,
tradition, the gnarled old yew
listing over generation X?
Family came in with scones;

off I drove. That night
I felt bereft, like a trespasser
who'd unwittingly soured
the very milk of loving-kindness.

18   Last Statement

Whatever I said, there hadn't been a hearing.
He was seen going out at first light
the very next day, the billowing
camouflage of fog on his untilled fields
becoming less poetic by the hour
as day shifted closer to land, and the facts;
his were the furrow, and gouty thoughts
opened out of damp black soil;
potatoes, stones, blood-veined crystals.

What I'd volunteered was an imposture
for a man who'd weathered drudgery
before and after rain, two wars,
his wife's dotage, the vet, and now me.
Son, the truth's a scarecrow
like Jeremiah in a field of cucumbers,
and there's no other way of planting neaps.
So leave me with my lack of tact,
the weedy rack of absolutes.

And come the spring, don't expect me
to visit mumbling about loss.
Look to your own. Work from the roots up.

19 A Lungfish

I went into the room
and everything had been laid out.
So I waited on the edge of the explosion.

It was some way to the albatross ocean.
A moon crater showed,
full of rain from the inland sea.

My hands were shaped like a poacher's
imploring, lost in the detail.
The salt crown came and made glad.

20 Knock and Maize

Sabbath recognitions flagged me down
ascending the switchback to the perennial square
of the high farm: its warmth and reek.

A road, a gate, a view of the sea
in the last place on earth.
Absentmindedly I retraced my own steps

with the few things a doctor can say
when things are complete, and the symbols gone,
and people foster a way of not-hearing.

In any case, I didn't speak enough
about the metaphors that started out as tiny boats
across the Irish Sea, distances

that could be heard in my brogue
and made me about as welcome as the bonesetter
or the travellers they sometimes took me for

hauling loose talk
of agues and serpentines
up the road from Columba's half-moon bay.

With my foot, I enjoined a stone to leave its epoch
and thought of the way pain works,
blunt figures of speech straining across the fields,

all process and outcome. A mission of joy,
I said to the dog, this doctor's life
going round doors, making folk feel at home.

21   Radiant Forms

You know the way out west, don't you? –

Past the notorious effluent, and the caravan convoy
parked at the chippy, through rushes, briers
and the long strip of goose grass, hardly
noticing the moon as it lays out
its strategy in the platitudinous old lake
troubled, if it ever was, by the twitch and slap
of frog spawn, helpless bog-cotton heads
blown clean across till they snag
on the verminous tire dump on the far side.

Spores of the god's breath, you weren't thinking –
nothing to interrupt your field of vision
as insistently as the city lights on a summer night;
stellar clouds of moths, makeshift airborne
flappers and tumblers, downdraughts of boreal air.
Stop. Stop and look across the bay;
and wonder why a chill blows off the sea
with its cache of drowned rationalists
and hard place on the strand, to this skewed station.

West is mighty circus talk, heaped clouds
above the whins and funnel-houses and granite
impediments. Lean over and drop,
no feeling in your feet, white faced one taken out,
roof on, and stored away with plaudits
and a musty pile of books. Fish for the mystery
in this old tin can of radiant forms, let it
dry on the change till you come back
peddling the language, like a mutter of swans.

I

Friesians marshalled behind blackthorns
gave way to perfect vision –
this was making do, this was radio on
and the song would be the old one
for as long as you like, without a sound.
It'll be a song about lost days.

II

A posse of quietly creeping guard dogs
stalked me across the field,
a mild alien displeased
to have caught his own hungry look
in their sheep-crazed eyes
and to have grasped its meaning.

III

Opening the gate I noticed treeborne gangrene,
ciliate echidniform closing-of-ranks,
placentas strewn across the whin
and on the sill,
like a trophy from the mud,
six fossil eggs wrapped in sea haar.

IV

This pig might have had wings
but he wasn't budging, stuck in the mud
and snorting at all those, like me,
who root for closeness.
His four cloven hooves said all there was
about possession and non-wings.

I didn't know how long I'd been there
in the stony quiet, knowing they'd pluck out
my pockets like flags of convenience
but let me walk away again
across that landscape
to find myself in the mercy of words.

A thrush startled at its descant.
There was that song again
unremarkable, even for farmers' wives,
a song about the sun's last rays
and birds out of Africa,
little dinosaurs that had taken wing.

23   *On Airyhemming Farm*

Those were some of the stories she knew,
errant, one-eyed, obsessional. Wooden clogs
of the same tradition. I was ignorant of
provenance, of name and thing
and the coiling parenthetical sentence sounds
that seemed a bodily straining upwards
out of mud, cement, the plummetless grasses.
I could have left, there and then,

but didn't. When the pain came she said nothing.
I sat among her personal effects
and waited for acknowledgement. I could hear
rain in the gutter, wind spilling
through the spruces. Once, penning the sheep,
she'd been struck by lightning. It sparked
sixty more years, till the rasp
of chronic illnesses. A cautionary tale,

but who would have stinted her that one exalting
moment on a hammock of turf –
to have seen a bucket fly and to get up herself,
black as sin, next to her charred sheep;
the walk back to the farm as if she'd stepped
over the hill and over the hill. God
in his implacable lair. Some small allure
to reach home and not rest till her life was done.

24   Mutations from Hafiz

Come back, Sun & Moon. Let me explain
why we have to scour the floor again,
hang a rung on the ladder, hope against hope

for friends' mild company and open prospects,
owls, cuckoos, the next half-century's
medusa-cities and our own quizzically anxious

retrievals of buckets and stars, the myth of shelter
glimpsed when it bolts from the glare
of things gone wrong, a small unmarked room

where Babel is being put back, bit by bit.
Sun & Moon, let me wake before my body moulds .
to those lumpy professional habits, mattresses,

old poultice packs. Under them is only what we
entered on: a carpet of soft sorrowing.

25   Sympathetic Healing

'Come with me,' said Asher, 'and you'll see it written in their eyes,
in their delinquent kids, in the way they sit and fidget on
        amphetamines.'

'You'd be that way too, if you lived in a rookery and kept the fire
        alive year in
year out, and watched light bluster from your life, as the pools
        predicted.'

I heard him talk, and heard the man on the other side boom over me,
sun behind his head, and a human figure beating down the strand
    with news of

nix. 'Thinking's only looks natural when there's nothing else to do.'
Sure enough, neither of us looked wiser with our fractals, chaos
    theory and black

box, the truants never once speaking of this or any other life
except one so high he wanted to stand up for himself, and move on out.

'Which is why,' Asher continued, 'of all the things you can do
the only one worth doing is to coax the jaw jaw, and let your fear

cross on the red. Why would you want to sit and watch stones
    grow? Art
starts with inadequacy, ours most of all. All you can do is listen.'

26 *Flight or Fright*

This was all the work of Nature, forked lightning
and the doc out on calls, all hours,
and the amazing heartlessness of guinea pigs.

You examined eyes for a lyric mood.
You checked the battery in someone's chest.
Standing in the wet, you addressed a horse's head.

No, this couldn't be anywhere near the city's edge.
This exhibited the patience of a superpastoral
where life was about standing still, even when working

and the hole got bigger and so did the risk.
Since you can't walk you'll have to fly, Just-the-Man.
Now if you can, if you can, if you can.

What was I doing in the country?
A chill wind came off the bay and fanned
through my clutch of hard principles.
Were they mine though? Or just clothes-hangers
I'd brought from my last job in the south?

Almost as far away across the dwindling bay
I could see lights coming on, local
fishermen on the Irish Sea. Early voyagers,
they knew the roar of the bathing pools,
blue lips, the aquarium shelving.

Tomorrow I'd be the man who disappeared.
Still, it was hardly a soft option, cajoling
cattle-drivers and settlers, gullible
landlubbers willing to indulge a head for heights.
Nothing stranger from my Jacob's ladder

than our new order, mornings when children
rose through sleep, tiny archaeologists
who showed me lichens and oxides, trailed
their fingers in my sense of time,
and found it hilarious, this losing footing.

28 *A Loss of Kind*

I
We talked of right, wrong, weather and the world.
Her body held no fuller form
than one rust petal plucked off from the sun.

II
It might have been a fabulous exchange of gifts.
Without a rose though, no ladder from the yard.
Help squalled like havoc in my hands.

III
This look has been abandoned by her eyes.
It is her body's proclamation of the fact.
I have to contradict it, but I can't.

IV
A loss of kind among the instruments.
Still the river leant beside her
lending an ear to what the tiger makes of man.

V
Now is then, the loss like nothing in the world.
What was the 'insult' in its yield?
No metaphor, just something kind can't mend.

29   Subjects and Objects

You couldn't agree more:
'The working life as a matter of conscience
and faith in one's fellow man.'

Not that you'd say so
early on a Monday, knowing this
must be the life you're having anyway.

But you touch yourself
gently at the kitchen sink, a reality show
of skiddery things called bodies,

more and more of them,
and all literal. Looks like you're
stuck now with the pictures.

Strange after the war
everyone should be healthy, unhappy
and longing for employment;

since, now there's no work left,
they'll probably tell us the future is imaginary
and has already been cancelled.

30   *Statistics for Beginners*

I opened the door on an estuary light discharging like the mind,
on lives easing in between quilts and quotes, glow-worms in the
    carbon dark,
an entire village shivering under the starryveldt of an oxidative storm,
rows of boggy ankles, diminished tidal volumes, stop gaps.

And the reasons were always bog-eyed, amazed at the world's analysis
of its own problems, rainy curtains and the light frotted gold,
and mine of their digitalised fluttering bird-hearts, stroked by my
    hand
as if to confirm them language was only ever a slow fugue.

I guess that's why the wind spat back the louder I shouted;
and one degree of freedom was all the freedom I had to lower the tone,
to put my mark on the west coast view of marram and men-of-war,
seaweed to dung the garden and an oyster-catcher's alarm.

And why I skated a while on the mundane egg, trying to make sense
of heroes and jokes and aftermaths, ripped feathers to the hunter
who stuffs thunder in a barrel, and trembles the lip of time
with his talk of hope, and a chance in twenty, as if he knows what's
    what.

★

Impediments

Micrologies, Proofs and Autobiographemes

> 'Nobody excluded the possibility that things could proceed in other, entirely different ways. You would have said that now each individual was ashamed of being the way he was expected to be'
>
> Italo Calvino, *Time & the Hunter*

1

Capture, recapture and maximum likelihood: those are my guiding principles on each excursion across the salty pavements of Paris to a room where I plot my three *points de repère*: M_1, M_2 and M_3.

2

In Charcot's room in the Pitié-Salpêtrière there is a wax model of a woman with her spine arched like an exocet. Her hand is draped across her body to the supernumerary rib indicated with a pointer.

3

Dissatisfaction follows me home, a fictive lack deliberating what it might have done before remorse charged the air of a bare room, a incongruous RAPPEL on the door recalling how to exit in a fire.

4

There is a parrot-loop on her ansaphone, like Diderot's pre-patent draft for a talking-machine. *'Est-ce que vous avez enfin trouvé votre bonheur? C'est la connaissance. C'est la connaissance.'*

5

A monumental blunder to let hunger go to my head listening to the cleaners at 2 AM, their raptors spraying disinfectant on the walls and on the stencil of Rimbaud purposefully striding off to Africa.

6

Hulled and planked, these are the boards of a funeral ship from the Louvre, every creak ricocheting back to the joiner who trued it to sail out of time, a craft persisting into utter perplexity.

7

A tidal volume, three atmospheres in the chest, air heaved out and hindered in its cavities, the alveolar honeycomb stringy with phlegm. Utterance: it shrinks like an oyster sprinkled with lemon.

8

All morning I discuss with you whether pain has any meaning. We list its synonyms in several languages: grief, sorrow, anguish, shame, guilt. Long Roman roads by which fathers enter sentience.

9

In the garret above me is Beckett's holy man, sucking on his last stone. I can't quite credit it, but he's tapping out a message on the floor. 'To have drunk of God from all His pitchers. Selah.'

10

Paris and its faubourgs, like every medieval city, resemble a kidney glomerulus, the river snaking through the inner citadel like the afferent-efferent collecting system of the loop of Henlé.

11

In the last instance, statistics are a form of wish-fulfilment. What can I do with that inwit, reading of Ahab's heroic swimmers-away? Or beside my colleagues, their pure stream of management?

12

The world and his wife are looking down on us from the Flood. Once the waters have drained, God will visit a far greater calamity on their offspring, ill-starring them like Ezekiel's cucumber growers.

13

Two biological totems of the C20: the Body-as-Armour, girding its loins to avoid being pierced through the soft point of its basilisk anatomy; the Body-in-Pieces, a vapour shower from the lip-sync.

14

An August day, in a tidal city, and a flying carpet from the Sahara deposits sand, grain by grain, on the courtyard. Then I remember: grace and rain – synonyms from the Abassid occupation of Atlantis.

15

Say 'I shall take hold of your antelope neck, blown-ember eyes, small-of-the-back-fitting fingers, thin-keeled ribs, rise-in-the-road pelvis' and have her, pointed daughter of the revolution.

16

Somewhere out in Boulogne-Billancourt is the hulk of the Renault factory where Simone Weil worked the shift for six weeks, before she got the bum's rush. Would she need to have written, 'Believe your pain'?

17

My method of arrival remained the same for years: disembarking from the coffin space of a couchette at the Gare de l'Est's songlines – 'Sticklers for detail/Toujours pointilleux' – before going off to work on the language.

18

He returns the original sense of mobility to tables and desks by throwing them out the window. Other mobiles follow: chairs, hat-stand, windowframe and door. The four bare walls he calls home.

19

Working for Karl Kraus's great-nephew. Odd having to English ion-couplings and chaste chromosomal pairings in a room window-wide above the cries of the rue St Denis. 'I want your body, and I want it now.'

20

Look, this place is really Laputa, floating above its own hypertrophic exuberance, the grid plan that de Tocqueville, of all people, predicted in 1837. With its peasant feet though, in a bowl of vinegar.

21

The last great battle of the symbol was fought at Valmy and observed by Goethe. In Year One of French Liberty a certain M. Brissot wrote: 'We cannot be calm until all of Europe is in flames.'

22

A curtain of rain decks old army routes, ribs of trees cut down at La Défense, the architectural uncanny and the roofs of Batignolles where, Kafka told his diary, Apaches are still on the loose.

23

Quaquaversalities, cornycracks of the metamidi, Scotch Reviewers' scotomata, gallusrictus, readywise read-mes, melimelos, sans-caniculottes, Desperantists, scotologicologophobists...

24

A city oozes in the arena making a holy show of history with the national razor: still not one step closer to redemption or the high water mark of 1848. An exposed nerve's blue disjunctive voltage.

25

At night I take Rilke's panther out of its gilded cage and let it drink at the remotest oases, from the Panthéon to the catacombs. In the morning it returns to its cage and locks the door behind.

26

Light spumes on the table, or falls like a stone. I've no use for it, detaching myself from the implications with something like fear, setting out over the Périphérique's endless traffic of abstraction.

27

The unit formula contains polyols, magnesium stearate, titanium dioxide (whitener), gum arabic (binding agent) and carrageenan, the only Gaelic word to enter the entire pharmacopoeia.

28

There is no cure for stammering, this manual says, except to fill your tongue with stones and let them weigh down your tongue, every quoi-que-ça-soit a bitter curse against language.

29

An expedition to the earth, abandoned for a hundred years, led by a suspiciously juvenile Tintin, the air thick with Captain Haddock's profanities. Blistering barnacles! The porters are sprouting feathers.

30

Bourg l'Abbé, Brady, Caire, Choiseul, Colbert, Grand-Cerf, Havre, Jouffrey, Panoramas, Prado, Princes, Puteaux, Verdeau, Vero-Dodat, Vivienne: all built on the coffee-grains of the 19th century.

31

He looks like a stateless ambassador or an Aztec fisherman dressed by Vesalius, the vena cava touched up with blue, the coeliac plexus with yellow. Under the sacking a toe-tag reads 'Honoré de B——'

32

Lift up your organs to an administrative level and listen to those mystical voices of the viscera: Dog Cadaver, Flabby Piss, Bird's Sex, Gluttonous Thief, Flying Fish, Filth, Stinking Lung. You old cerealist!

33

I meet the Historian in the metro and he sprays tear gas in my eyes. I meet him in one of the Passages, and he tells me to relearn hopscotch. In the Musée d'Orsay, he shouts 'Wake up, dunderheid.'

34

Queen Quintessence is still living in the modest rue d'Ecosse, hard by the Panthéon. True to kind, every Saturday she has her maid put a sum on the 3:30 at Longchamps. One of a cohort of panicky quaggas.

35

A jute basket of bees squirms on the outside wall, a last symbol of the guilds. Of our solar civilisation, what's left is a scarab pushing a dung-ball, industry clothed in its own possibility.

36

In this basin, dreams dribble into the vortex like mercury and give off pungent vapours, a great collective sink where the individual dream has the same specific gravity as a trickster's urine.

37

What's in Pandora's box? Peleus' javelin appropriated by Achilles, Hercules' lion's-paw pectorals, the aegis tattooed around Athena's chaste aureole, Hermes' caduceus, Hades' toejam, Zeus' jism.

38

To take a leaf from Rabelais' book. Paris' marriage of architecture and amnesia takes two names: '*Lutetia*, meaning city of mud (*lutum*) and *Parisis*, city of Iris, mysterious sidelong goddess of truth'.

39

Anatomically, the spinal column extends from the seminal vesicles to the cortex immediately posterior to the seas of cinnabar and surfactant: the ideal conduit for a series of animals in harness.

40

When I come to outlier M_n I know how much scatter to attribute to my near-Gaussian distribution of observation points. Divide it by the mean, and there it is: a coefficient of variation.

41

The Revolution has an address: 232, rue Saint-Antoine. What else but Gothic *cerceri d'inventione* where the carrier-pigeons were trained to drop their calcium-enriched messages on the governor's cucumbers.

42

Suppose there to be n equally possible outcomes to an action and the event e is n_e of these outcomes. In probabilistic terms, success is encapsulated by the term n_e/n, failure by $n-n_e/n$.

43

Hemmed in by this brute of an existence but still clinging onto the Raft of the Medusa for dear life, he offers it an oath of fealty, waiting for calamity to act on him like some sublime sunset.

44

Carragheen. Irish seaboard town. Structural polysaccharide of red seaweed (*Rhodophyceae*). Consists of alternating copolymers of galactose, commonly used as a gelling agent, emulsifier and stabilizer.

45

When you wake up at noon, you feel like the homunculus of the sensory cortex remembered by every medical student: preponderant rough tongue, pulpy prehensile monkey grip, colossal genitalia.

46

A corset, a portfolio of dirty postcards, a hideous stuffed parakeet, a chincilla scarf, studlinks, wooden clothes-hangars, shoe polish, a Napoleonic scabbard. The terrible din when phenomena come to speech.

47

The Lord is my Personal Adjustment Logical (PAL). He leadeth me through the categories of DSM IV to Joyce's grievous mournings around the fall of a leaf. A leaf like any other leaf.

48

DEFENSE DE REVER (*loi du 29 juillet 1889*). And should you dare to, you'll be frogmarched down one of Haussmann's spacious avenues to meet the Angel of Mons kitted out by Marcel Duchamp.

49

How easily fish take on the shapes of ideas, defiant to the last cartilaginous spicula. The horror, one morning, licking the salt from her skin, to find one still flapping on the pillow, its gills still sucking air.

50

A dizzy view of M_x: Lisa Foussagries 'conquérant' Paris as she hangs from a strut of the Eiffel tour, clad in a Lucien Lelong dress. M_y: an angel over Dresden in ruins, a mere six years later.

51

Her forehead opens like a drawer when she bends forwards to comb her hair, spilling a fig, pomegranate seeds, some dust from the turmeric red plains of the Euphrates, our little sister with no breasts.

52

A person trades a name with another person. For example, Hard-Two-Rains exchanges his with No-Hut-No-Name but has to give him a bottle of Lagavulin because of the desirability of the name.

53

Enkidu was still living in a mattress and tyre when Miss Stein took a Hopi primer and announced to the first sailor to disembark after the war, here is here and there is no there there.

54

One of uncle Siegfried Löwy's favourite sayings, scribbled down by adolescent Franz in a morocco notebook: 'Writing prescriptions is easy, but reaching an understanding with people is hard.'

55

The pronunciation of 'r' as a topology of origins in Europe. Mine not phlegmy or throaty, but the clear-water border burr of Sir Walter holding on for dear life to Jenny Deans' petticoat frills.

56

Mayhew walked straight out of the Church Lane swag-shop and over to gay Paree where he could observe naked men swimming in urine, one every now and again diving into the swill to rescue a fish-head.

57

Eczema smooches with Halitosis. Kyphosis pays a round for Prostate. Paraplegic is a war veteran. Who couldn't fail to admire you, the flagellant of individual phenomena, overstanding the afternoon in Café Expressioniste?

58

Raise one eyebrow in the manner of the aristocracy (superficial temporal muscle) during the Reign of Terror and you'd find your cranial nerves radically disjunct from your means of escape.

59

The sober little roof of the circumflex on the word 'honnête' makes it immediately suspect. Not to mention the snake hidden underneath which keeps popping out to prick the conscience.

60

Talleyrand the Magnificent steps out of the Upanishads of European history on a white charger, a man described by the Duchesse d'Abrantè as 'having betrayed everything except style'.

61

Expériencer, expérimenter: the same word, the same motor of the modern, just as the sacrificial world organized itself around the swelling track of the mother-rivers, Rhine and Rhône.

62

Passing by the Bir-Hakeim bridge, a petulant reedy bandoleon wheezes on an upper floor. Another last tango, but the first in Paris was surely Buñuel's sound track for *Un Chien Andalou*.

63

Her room has the odour of processed chrysanthemums and dead anthropods, (1R cis)S- and (1S cis)R-enantiomer pair of (alpha)-cyano-3-phenoxybenzyl-3-(2,2-dichlorovinyl)- 2,2-dimethyl-cyclopropane carboxylate.

64

What should we make of the absence of jokes in the Old Testament? That jokes are saboteurs? That being outwitted would bring the wind of laughter howling across the Negev as purest loss?

65

Clinical signs of poisoning starting at 3 h post-dose were piloerection, diarrhoea and crouched posture; abnormal gait, epiphora, fasciculation, tremor, tachypnoea and lack of grooming were also observed.

66

Qdm: the East. *Cadmus*, the man from the East, dragging the bull's head Aleph behind him, boustrophedon up the terraces of language to a janitor's job in BHV or the Kaufhaus des Westens.

67

In Sudre's Solresol (Langue musicale universelle of 1817) *misol* expresses good, *domisol* God, and *sollasi* to ascend. Casting down the devil is a silasolo solmido in strictest stretto.

68

Dido, Xwarši and Qapuči: these are ghost-towns on the banks of the Andi and Koissou, seed-husks, no excrement, only a young boy showing where to wade the rivers across.

69

She had her children under road-signs. They comforted her against the bald truth. They simplified her fate. They were all superlatives, and she wouldn't allow them to abandon her.

70

'By faith, Noah oracularly warned of concerning things not yet seen, moved with fear, prepared an ark for the saving of his house; by which he condemned the world...' Hebrews 11:7

71

Having chosen to stay above ground, you let fear of your sad office drive you into the vitals of a whale: If only you could confess to the whale why you had to leave so much and go towards so little.

72

My mother purling the grey seams back into the sunset, assuages her worries about my welfare with a cup of tea. Son, she would say, it's as much difference as you'll ever find between here and there.

73

They lead you out into the yard to shoot you. You notice some old bricks, turds, a broken coop, pocked plaster. You write your last words on a scrap of paper and they stuff it into your mouth.

74

Whole dishes become extinct, under a fur of ergot. I was amazed that you rose steaming from the hamam, mouth full of mealcake, to savour my aspirated national dish: *al-hisa' al-iskotlandi*.

75

I have a charm of nine joys and distilled figwort for the cold gravel disease that bothers you, but on the way out don't forget to offer a glass of water to the god of ladders, charm being alien to descent.

76

In the flat on the Ile St Louis where you slipped her a yard. Or the other one in St Sulpice, listening to the bells go Bim Bam Bom. All of that for the love of Shem the Penman's wife's pizzled quotatoes.

77

The room in the rue d'Enghien is entirely bare, the philosopher having ejected the contents. Only he interpreted what was left, the vestment of the four bare walls, as a kind of plenitude.

78

The city sudsides into four qualities: incandescence poising over its own decay, the ghetto's waxy ear, a continuous blue hum of foreboding, fear brushing the face like a fly's wing.

79

Was that it then? – A lone figure hunting in his wastebin to find where reality might be after the years of devastation, Teddy Wiesengrund writing us all off with a withering supremely grand gesture.

80

Even the sterilized white glazed tiles of a Casualty Department can't keep out the heteroclite outrageous images conjured up by Extract of Ipecacuanha, used to induce vomiting in children who've been given presents.

81

One night I dreamed of running my childhood again from Langside to Crossmyloof, the exact route of Mary Stuart's rout after the battle, that moment of truth in 'England's' destiny.

82

In another locus of the possible, the river of life opens out like a grand piano with half the keys missing, oblivious to the four elements: the law of shit, time in arrears, mirky nights, blood squeaking on the tiles.

83

Dr Knock's practice has grown so big that his method has been imitated by every doctor in the Sécurité sociale. The secret of his success: awarding each patient his or her very own disease.

84

When he heard her story it put him to shame. The shame got up and followed him from the room. Then it careered across the world, and all he could do was nourish himself on its diminishing hoofbeats, all one horse.

85

Mr Beckett got up and called the nurse, having seen enough, and nothing out of the ordinary, just the terrible things again; first light, streets sleeked with rain, the day's dispersals of pigeons.

86

According to a report from the Compagnie des Eaux the average Parisian drinks the 'same' glass of water seven times before it joins the Seine's meander to the sea, distal to Haussmann's green Cloaca Maxima.

87

I made a desert in my mind, at the world's end. It was the perfect antipode of Paris. The heat was a deadly assailant. There I watched Benjamin come out at night and water the signposts.

88

Enkidu came out of the bush and lived in the great city. One day he would take off his shoes in the House of No Return. First he would live in the city until the city became strange to him.

89

Excision repair (cut and patch): a chemical lesion recognised by endonuclease is excised by exonuclease, the DNA degraded and the missing part of the strand resynthesized by polymerase.

90

Professor Y descends into the city's entrails, a soft blue RATP ticket in his hand and takes the Number 1 line to La Défense. Dites donc! a hawker selling his ideas, shiny green avocados, galley-slave catarrh.

91

You pick up your feet and begin to run. You run and run, and the road loosens your muscles, wings your stride, such a broad avenue, would run you quite out of the world, were it not for a pebble in your shoe.

92

The very hand of Providence brought me up in the vaults of the British Linen Company's bank, in the north end of the Untied Kingdom, assessing the Book's stringent monoculture.

93

One tradition disappeared into a trenchcoat to glower with intent. The other ravaged round from Skaggerak to Ushant on its flat Friesian vowels. God, sadly, was the word that failed them both.

94

Crossmyloof? We were foraging for accent and haleness, wrapped in rain and listening to the trade winds bruising the thistle. Which is where I repay the filial debt by stroking the palm of Ingrès's violin.

95

A wet landscape spoke before I could read what answer it had sent to the forum of tight little nations, each one huddled round the hearth, a mutual admiration society outmanoeuvring the other's armistice with history.

96

L'Illustration's picture report featured the assassination of the Austrian crown-prince by a Serb in between storm-damage to the Saint-Augustin quarter and the Pierreries ball of the Duke and Duchess of Gramont.

97

Once out of your sweatbath, I towelled you down with my wing feathers, annointed you with hyssop and hummingbird tallow. You sealed my heart, like a daughter of Jerusalem, with the roof of your mouth.

98

Some common acronymic parameters. Forced expiratory volume in t seconds (FEV_t). Mean residence time (MRT). Musil's standard European psychic unit (SEPU). Kristeva's obligate jargon index (OJI).

99

Maxims of the Inzwischenzeit. Time to make light of hard work. Time to deplore the scandal of the future tense. Time to leave the library. Time to run against the rock stuck in the way.

100

His cuneiform marginal markings couldn't grasp their own meaning: childish ribbons of laughter, the destroying angel's access to hope, strangeness to the facts, and God bestriding the thick world of appearances.

101

Impedimenta. A land full of unlikeness where the people chew mint to freshen their breath, of giants and blasphemers, and many demented elderly. Of formal gainsay, mountains and one-word mystics.

Unsystematic Anatomy

after Rabelais

The vault of his cranium was an ordinary day shouting from the door
and his forehead was a drawer of objections
and his pineal was a big bellows
and his irises were Geminids on an bush evening
and his eardrums were tight skeins of geese
And the auricle of his ear a leaf stroked by Kafka in 1910
and his uvula was Benny Lynch's punchbag
and his saliva was a come-on
and his tongue was the negotiation of sweat-bath rituals.
His gullet was snake's knowledge
and his thyroid was the shield over Patroclus
and his recurrent laryngeal nerve was a prize-winning dissection
and his trachea was a ladder to the gods.
His spinal cord was all the news in sixty seconds.
His diaphragm was a bivouac on Cul Mor
and his lungs were the creature from the lagoon
and his liver was sitting all alone
and his gallbladder was the prodigal returning
and his mesentery was enough said about Boolahoola
and his spleen was the history of Belgium
and his stomach was pots and pans
and his small intestine the scarf that strangled Isadora Duncan.
His vena cava was the Third Man
and his mitral valve was a fond attachment
and his aorta was the Twenty-Third Psalm sung in the Hebrides
and his heart was an artichoke.
His kidneys were Pliny on recycling
and his ureters were double bungee jumpers reclining
and his bladder was a seat at the Citz watching the Chalk Circle
and his spermatic cords were a strung violin
and his penis was done on a dare.
His hips were titanium-vanadium, where the angel touched,
and his perineum was a canvas big top
and his pelvis was Lear's fool
and his femurs were a dream of being next in command
and his calves were pay first, touch later
and one foot was a Lisbon lion
and the other took a while.

His memory was laminar germ theory
and his commonsense was seasick in the heart of Europe
and his imagination was an open cast
and his thoughts were English composition and rhetoric
and his conscience was a lease on a bird cage in the Walled City
and his appetite was Boswell's inkhorn
and his hope was one for the road
and his undertakings were Daedalus and Icarus in the maze
and his will was the Cape of Good Hope
and his desire was the wounds of possibility
and his judgement was Solomon's treatises on deep tongues
and his compassion was undergrowth
and his discretion was beached, between herring and seaweed
and his reason sat down to turn itself in

in the gap between the boyhood burning of his ears
and finally arriving as himself.